African Am... in History

Stanford Makishi

Contents

Rigby®

A Harcourt Achieve Imprint

www.Rigby.com
1-800-531-5015

Matthew Henson

Matthew Henson was an important African American explorer.
In 1909 he made a trip to the North Pole.
He was one of the first people to reach this part of the world.
He wrote a book about the trip in 1912.

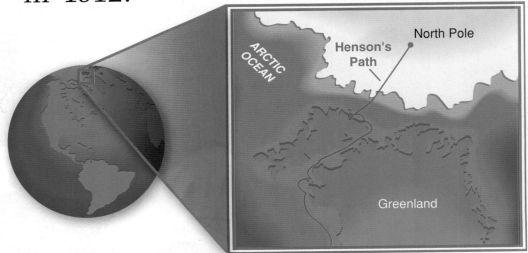

ARCTIC OCEAN

North Pole

Henson's Path

Greenland

5

Jackie Robinson

I learned about Jackie
Robinson, too.
He was a great baseball player.
Before 1947 African
Americans couldn't
play on Major
League baseball
teams.
Jackie Robinson
was the first African
American player
to do so.

ROOKIE OF THE YEAR

19 47

JACKIE ROBINSON

Martin Luther King, Jr.

I learned about Martin Luther King, Jr. He wanted African Americans to have the same rights as other Americans.

He wanted to change laws that
were not fair.
He gave speeches and led marches.
And the laws changed!
I'm glad he and so many others
worked so hard.

Barbara Jordan

I also learned about
Barbara Jordan.
She was the first
African American woman
from the Southwest to
become a leader in our
government.
She fought for
the rights of
many people.

Mae Jemison

I learned about Mae Jemison.
She was the first African American
woman to go into space.
She went on the space
shuttle in 1992.

I'd like to ride on
the space shuttle
someday!

13

Honoring Great African Americans

All of these people have helped make the world a better place.

I try to honor them every day.
Each day, I try to make our world
a better place, too!

Index